The Teacher's Gift

Dana Cretsinger

Illustrated by Alyson Murray

PALMETTO
PUBLISHING
Charleston, SC
www.PalmettoPublishing.com

The Teacher's Gift
Copyright © 2023 by Dana Stephens Cretsinger

All rights reserved
No portion of this book may be reproduced, stored in a retrieval system,
or transmitted in any form by any means–electronic, mechanical, photocopy,
recording, or other–except for brief quotations in printed reviews, without
prior permission of the author.

First Edition

Hardcover ISBN: 979-8-8229-2497-0
Paperback ISBN: 979-8-8229-2498-7

To Desi & Estus:
I wish for you both to always love the holidays—
no matter how tired and cranky the world or its people
might get. I hope you always look for the hidden
kindness others display and pay it forward. Xoxo

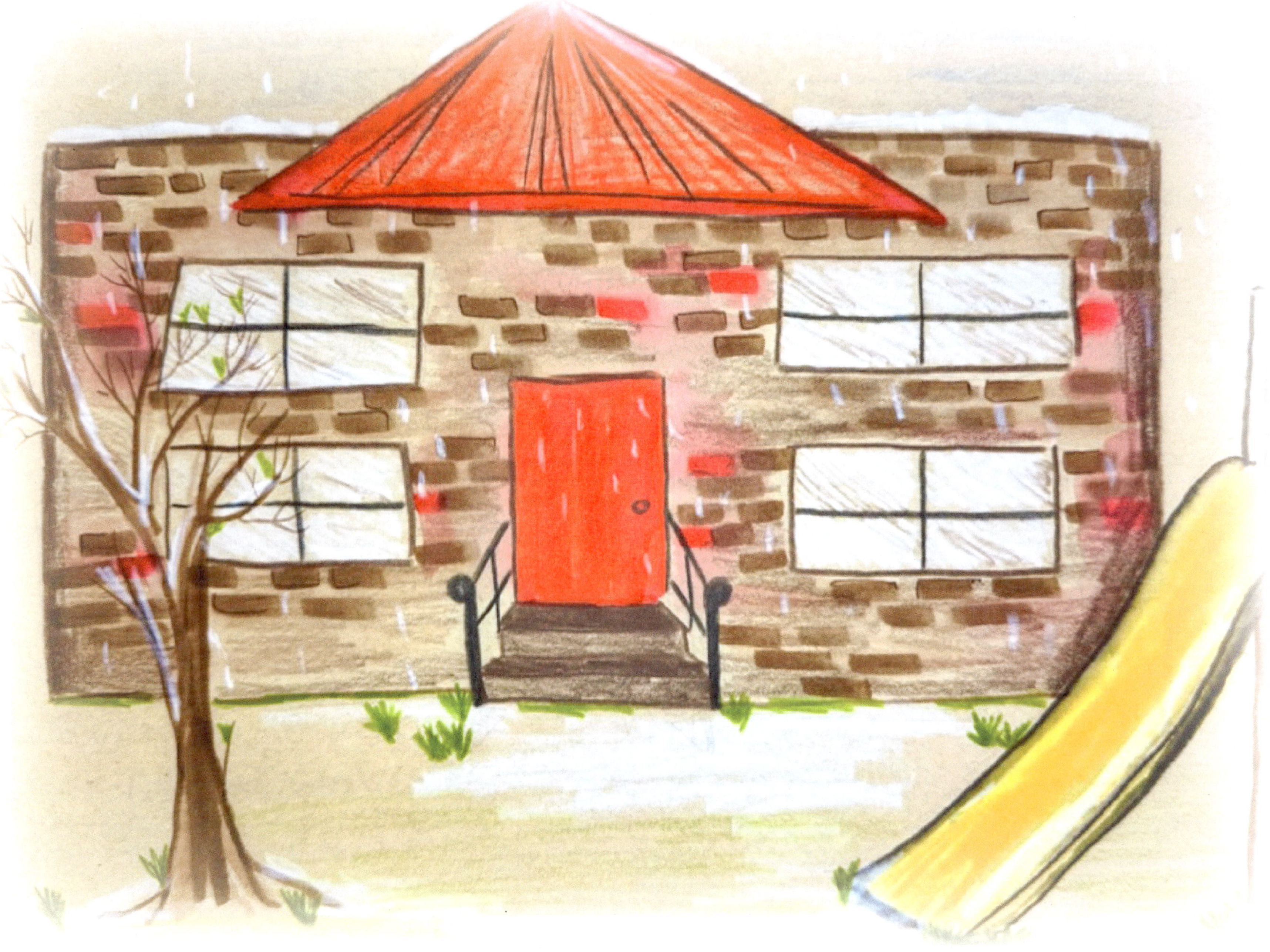

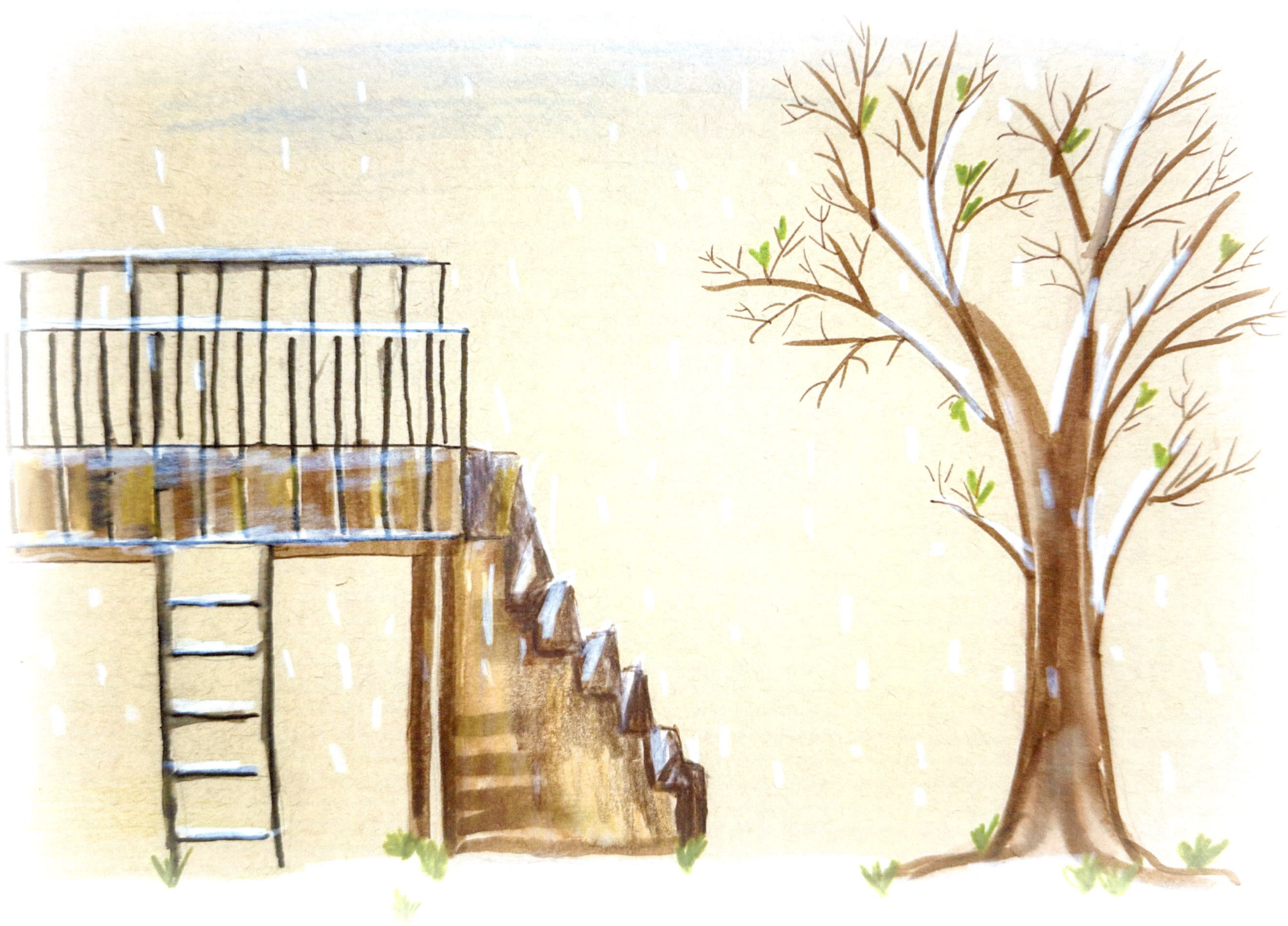

When the weather turns chilly, and snow falls from the sky to blanket the ground, you will always find the smile a bit brighter on the face of The Little Schoolhouse's first-grade teacher, Ms. Diaz.

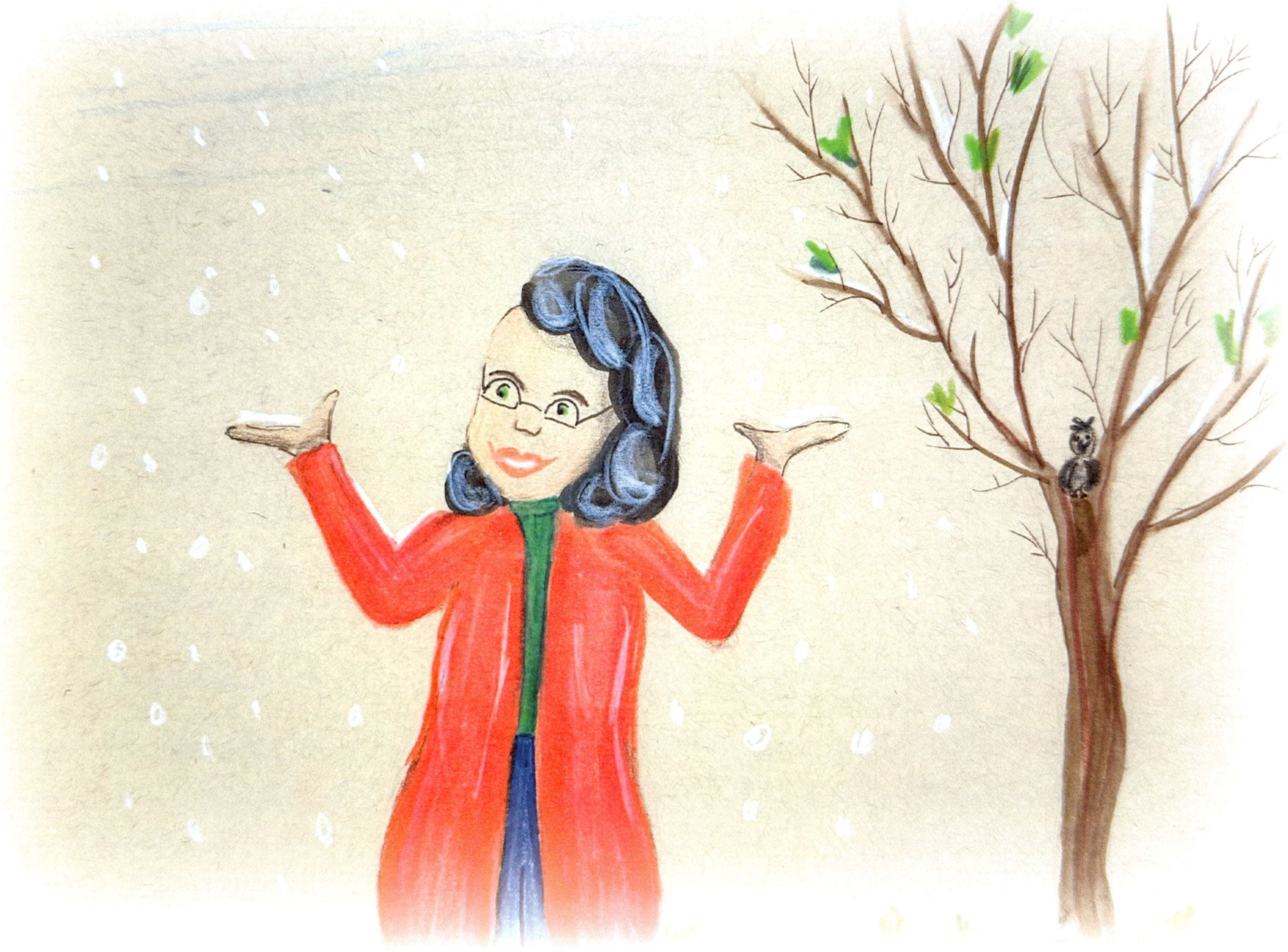

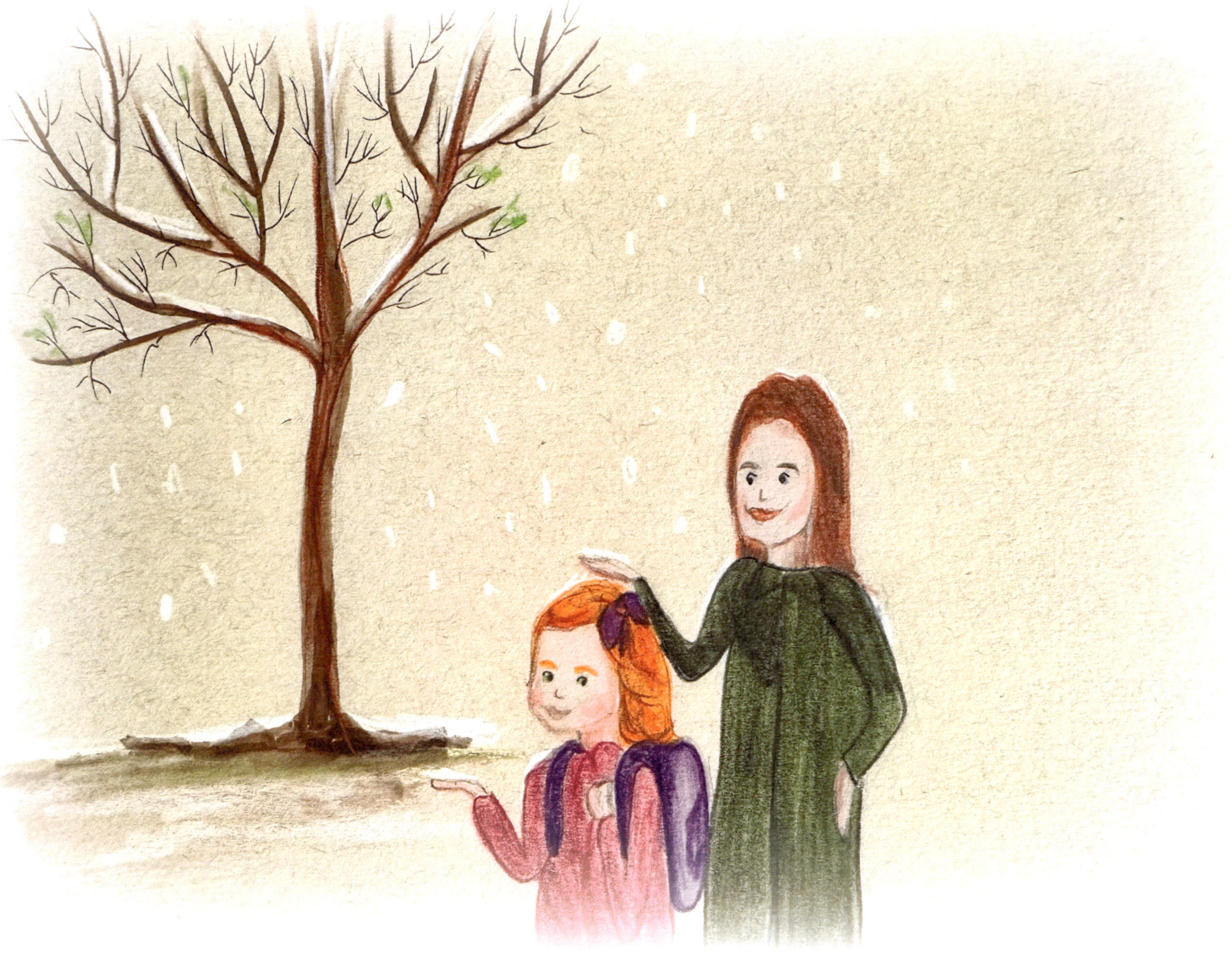

Considering how much Ms. Diaz smiles, that says a lot! Her smile is so bright that it inspires her students—and even their parents—to smile more!

DECEMBER
M T W T F S S
1 2 3 4 5
6 7 8 9 10 11 12
13 14 15 16 17 18 19
20 21 22 23 24 25 26
27 28 29 30 31

What is the reason for her smile being brighter, you ask? If you look closely at the calendar, you'll see that it is the month of December. For boys and girls, that means that winter break is near, but for Ms. Diaz, it means the holiday season is approaching—her favorite time of year.

Ms. Diaz loves everything about the holidays. She loves how the season inspires people to give to one another and be a little kinder than before. The very second that Thanksgiving has ended, you can be sure her classroom is decorated with snowflakes and gingerbread houses.

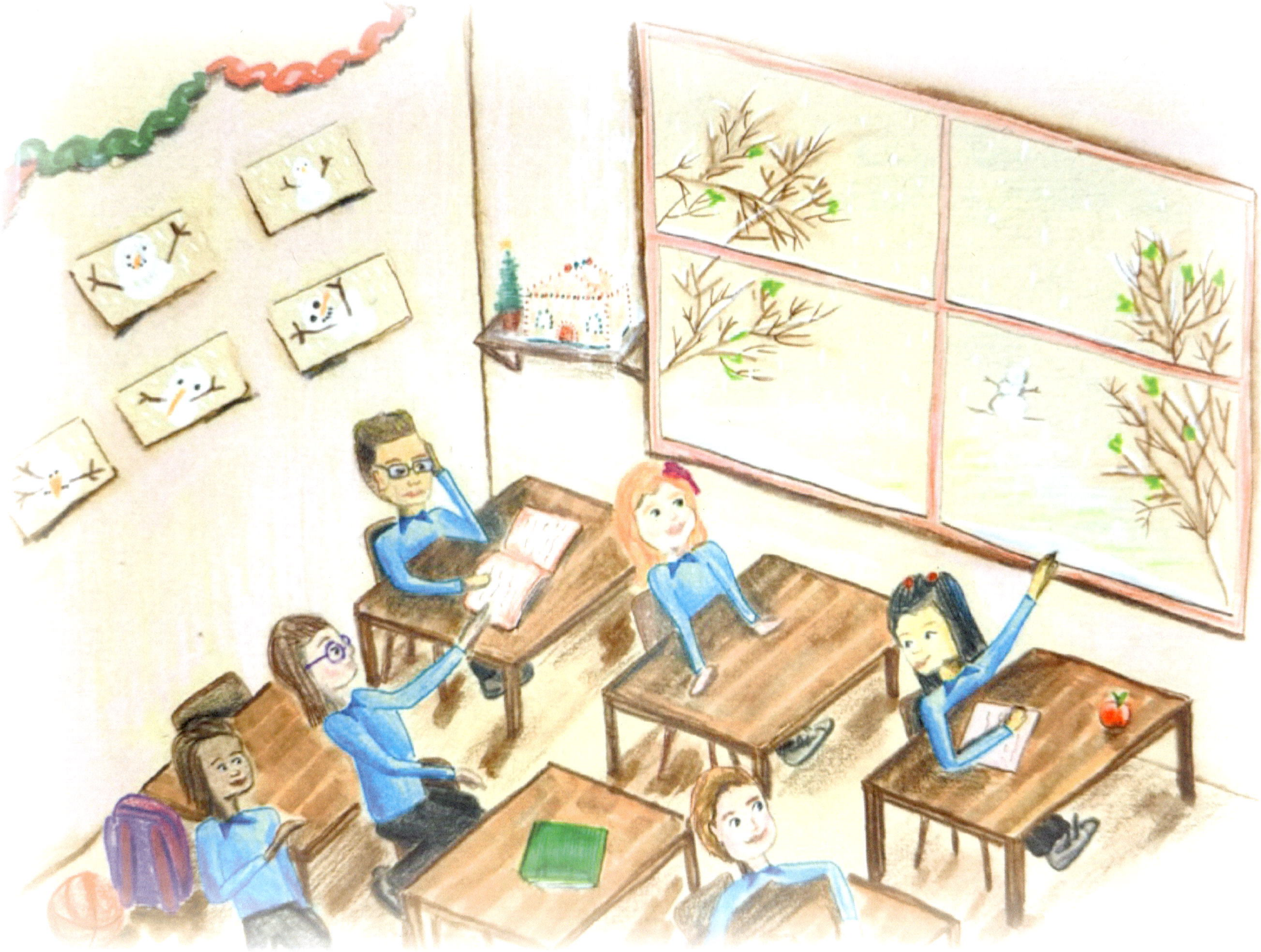

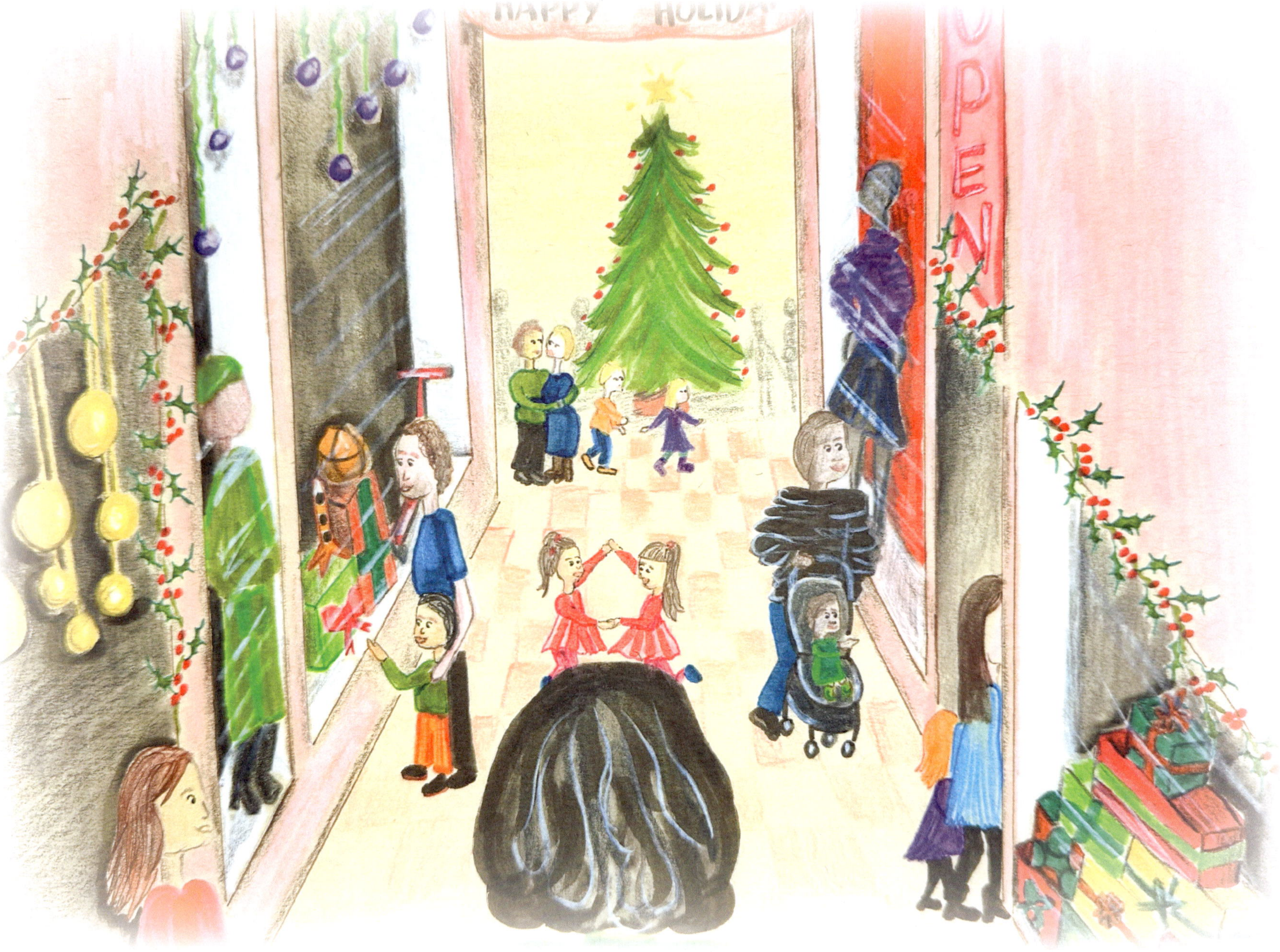
HAPPY
OPEN

While most people try to steer clear of the holiday crowds, not Ms. Diaz! She loves to stroll by all the stores just to look at the beautiful window displays. She watches the children's eager anticipation as they shop with their families for presents, and she loves to see the joy on their faces when they find something special!

There is only one thing Ms. Diaz loves more than the holiday season, and that is being a teacher.

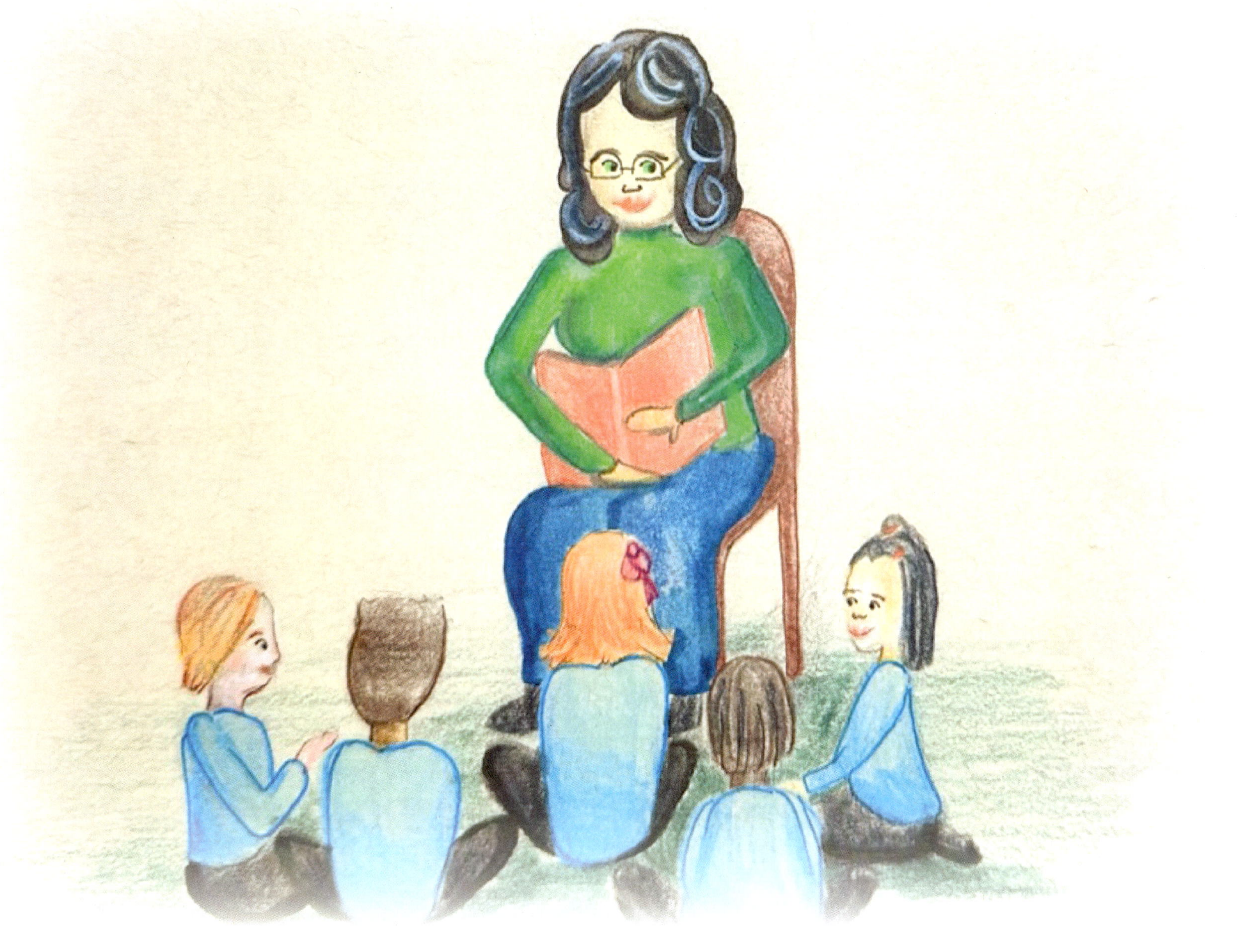

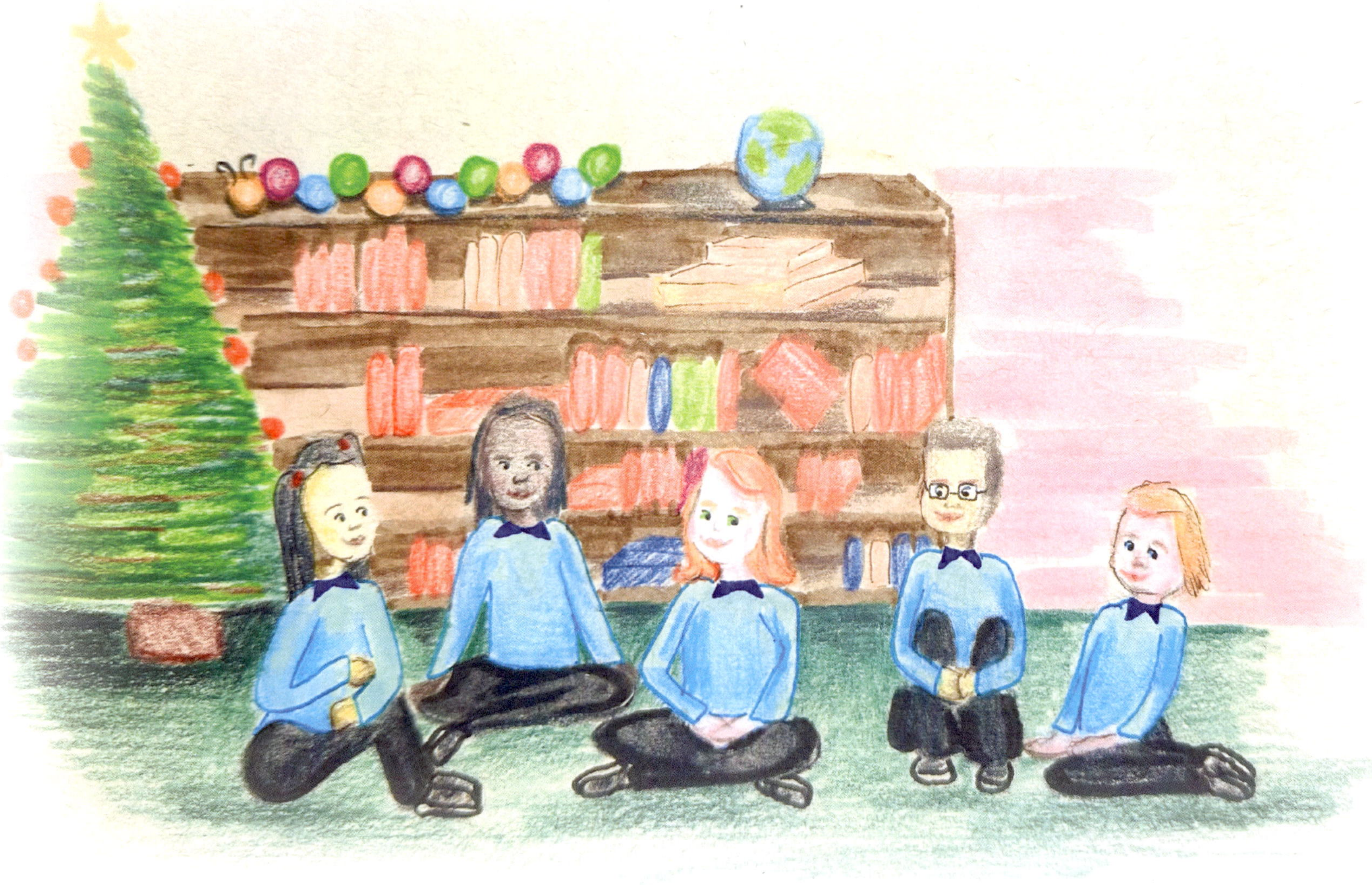

Ms. Diaz finds it magical to look at the faces of her first graders and see the glimmer of excitement in their eyes when the weather gets cooler. In her many years of teaching, she feels a special cheer in children's hearts as the holidays get closer.

Every day, she plans something special for her class—sometimes, it is a winter craft or a winter-themed story to read aloud. Ms. Diaz loves teaching so much.

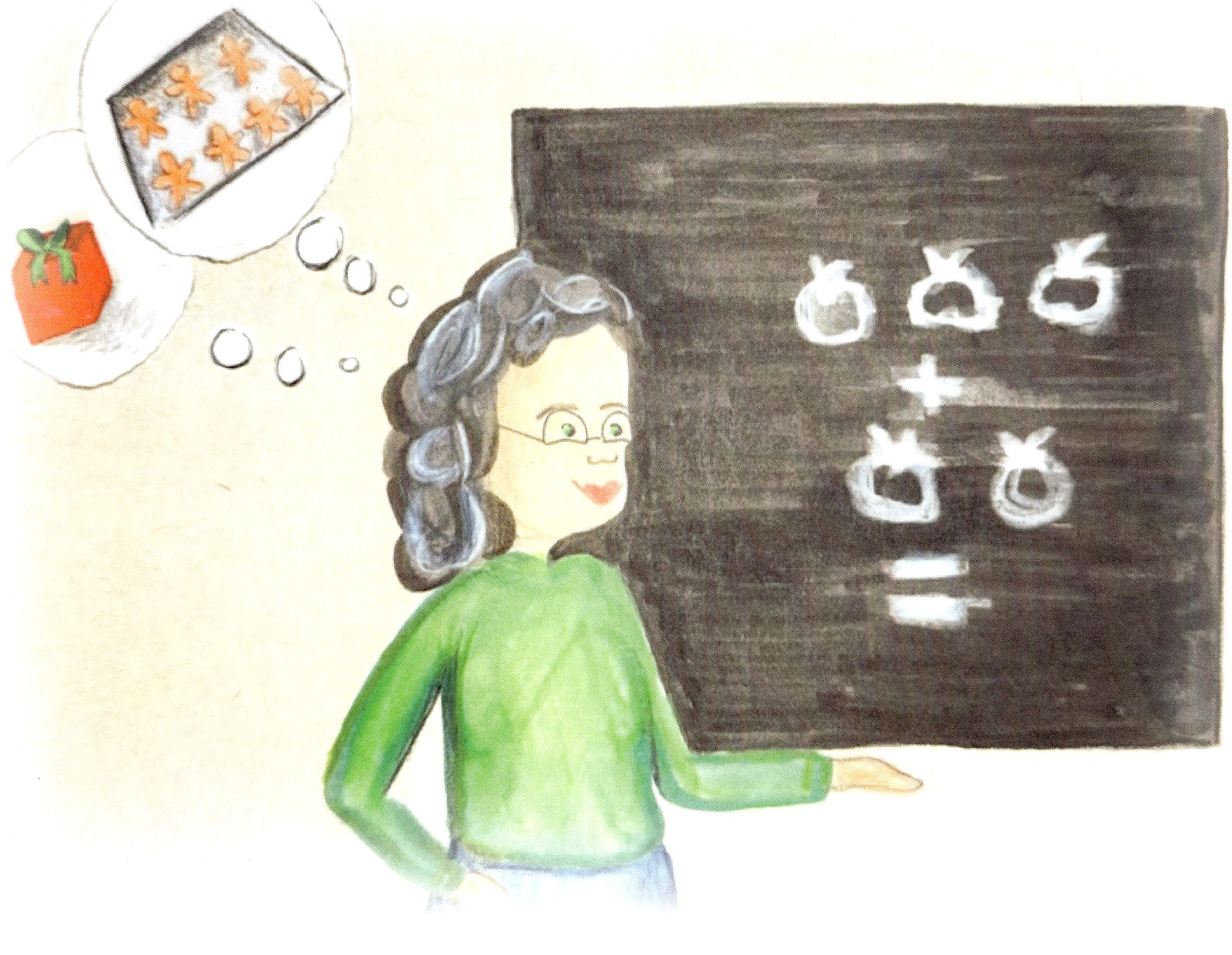

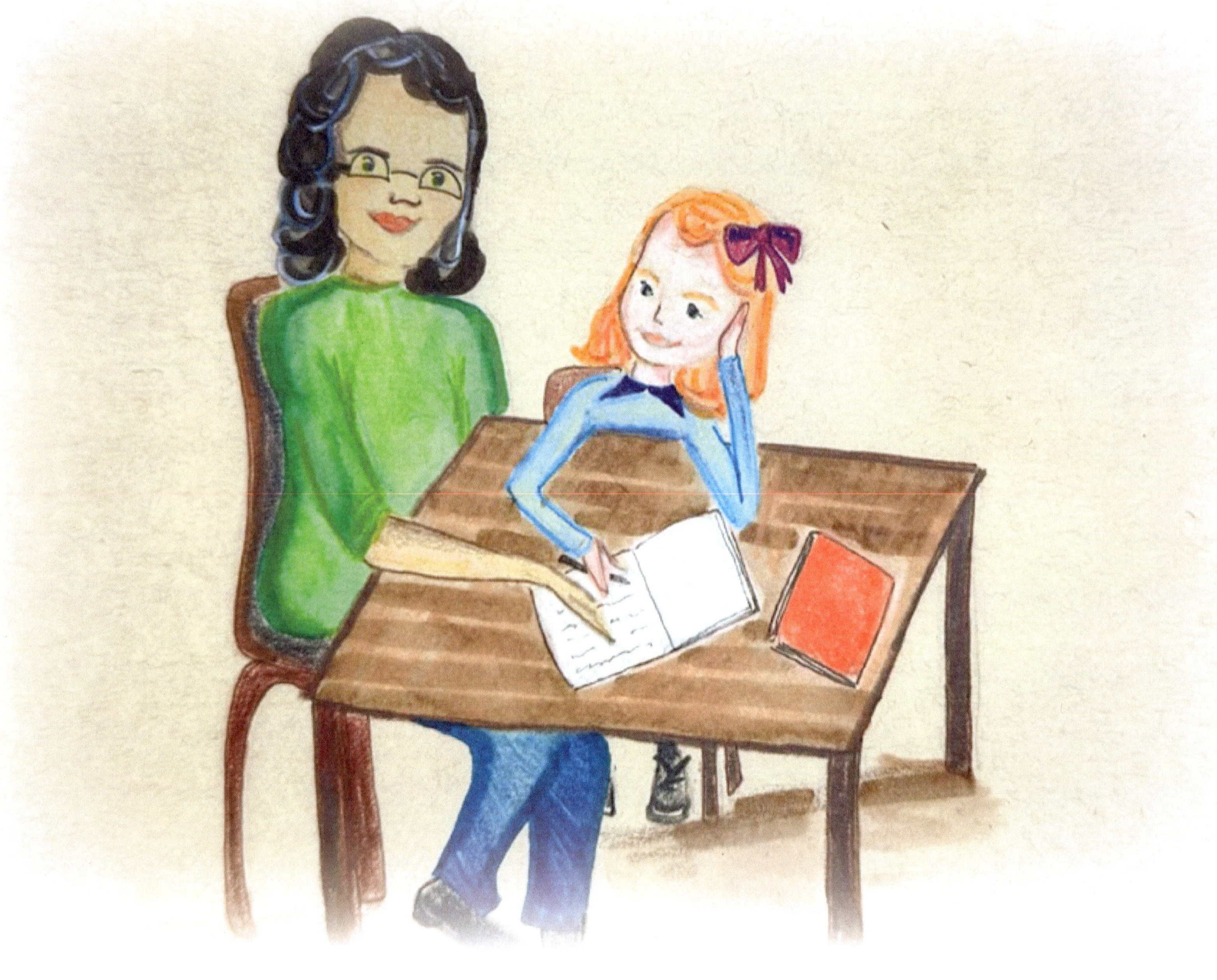

After school is over, Ms. Diaz stays late to tutor students. When she goes home, she bakes loaves of pumpkin bread to give to people and to share with her students the next day.

One frigid December day, Ms. Diaz noticed that one of her students, Nicholas, had again forgotten to bring a lunch and wear a coat to school. "Why, Nicholas! Aren't you hungry, and where is your coat?" Ms. Diaz asked. Nicholas, noticing the eyes of his class on him, replied quietly, "I'm not very hungry today, ma'am." Ms. Diaz felt there was more to the story, but instead of asking him again, she told him, "Well, I brought too much food for myself today. Would you help me by eating some so it doesn't go to waste?" She gave him her soup and some pumpkin bread at lunch, and Nicholas was happy to help her not waste food.

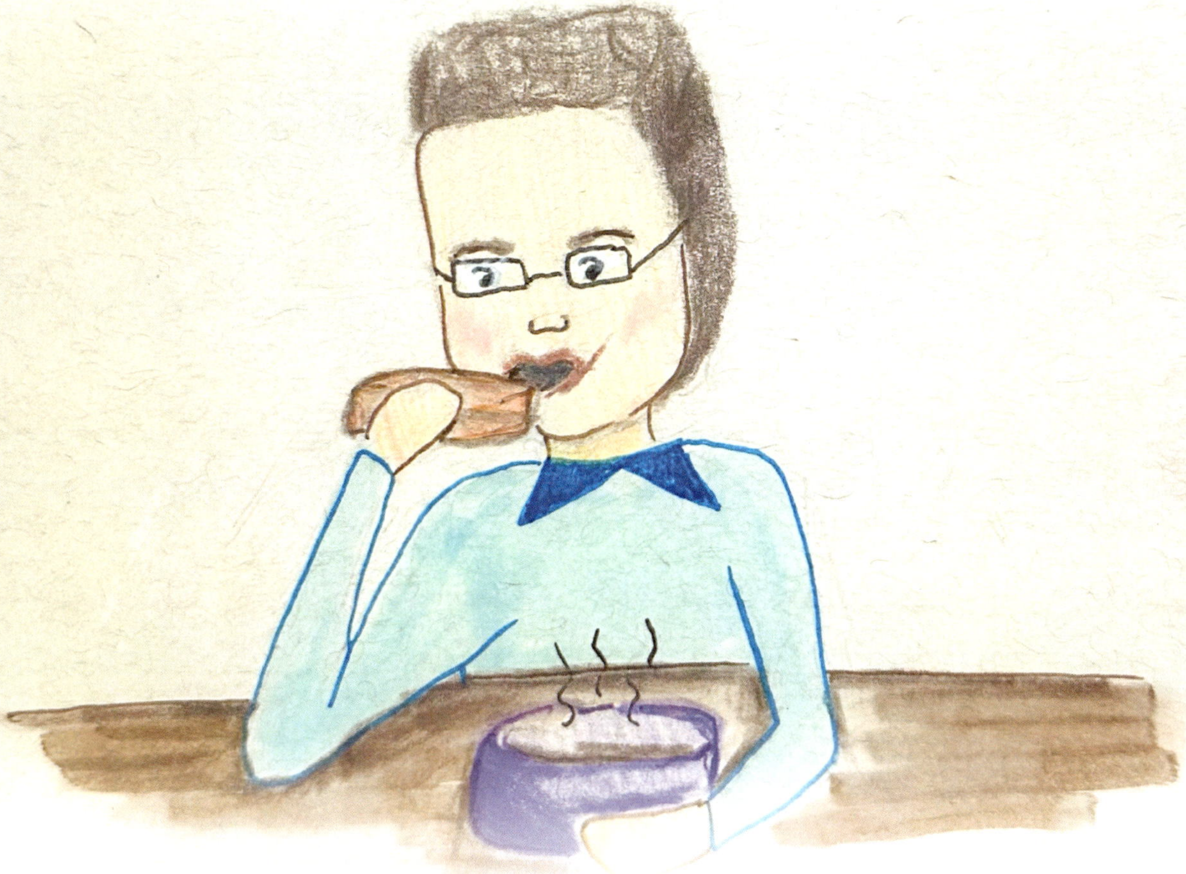

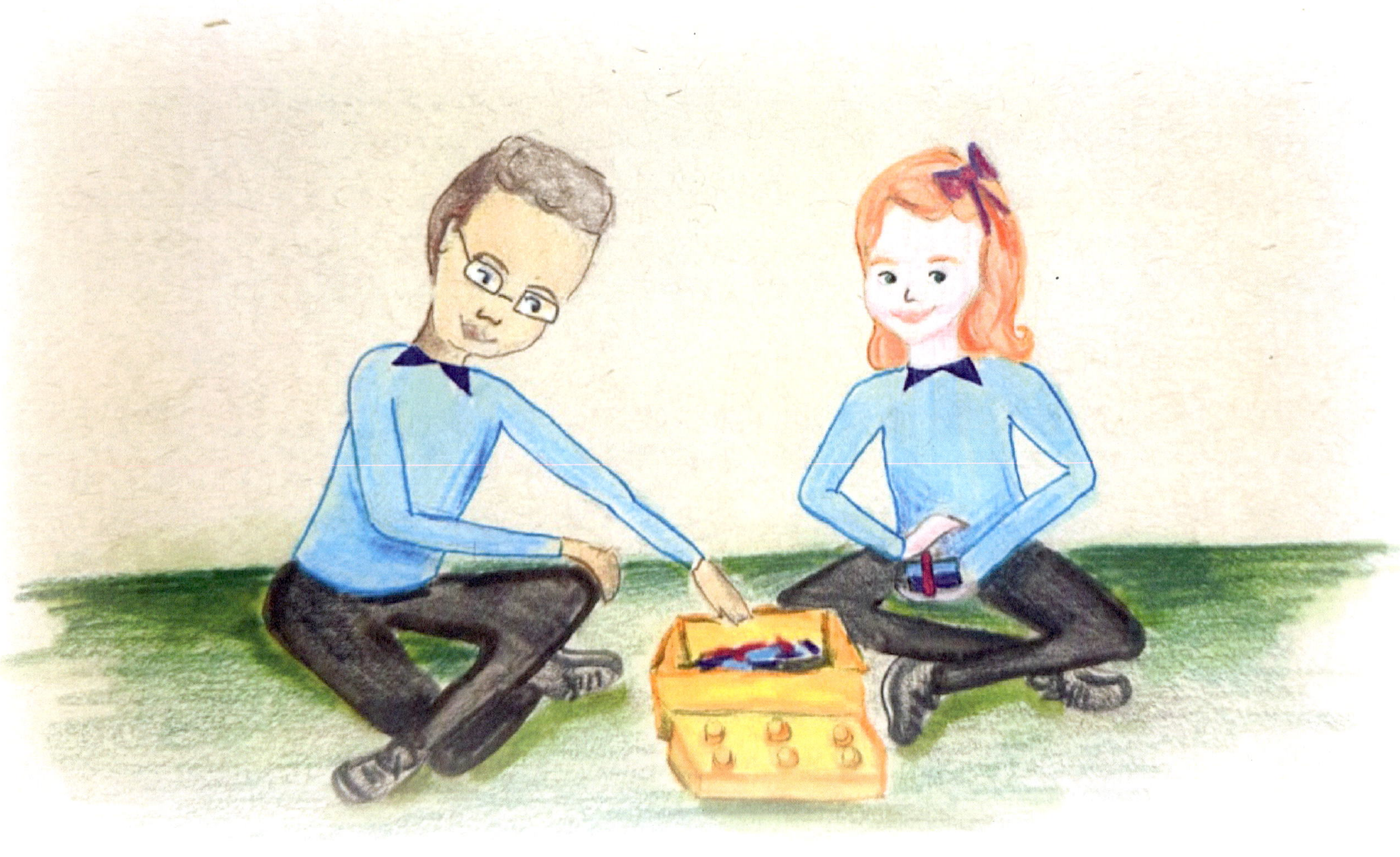

When it came time for recess, she asked Nicholas to be her special helper and told him he could also ask a friend to help. Special helpers erased the chalkboard for the teacher and then were free to color or play inside as they wished for the remainder of the break. He picked his buddy, Desi, and after they erased the chalkboard, they played with LEGO bricks while the rest of the class was outside.

That same day, after all the students were dismissed, Ms. Diaz prepared the classroom for the holiday party that was to take place the next day. Ms. Diaz had no tutoring sessions and planned to shop in town. Though she had been looking forward to her shopping trip all day, she couldn't stop worrying about her student forgetting his lunch and not bringing a warm coat to school. During the entire trip to the store, Ms. Diaz kept thinking of Nicholas.

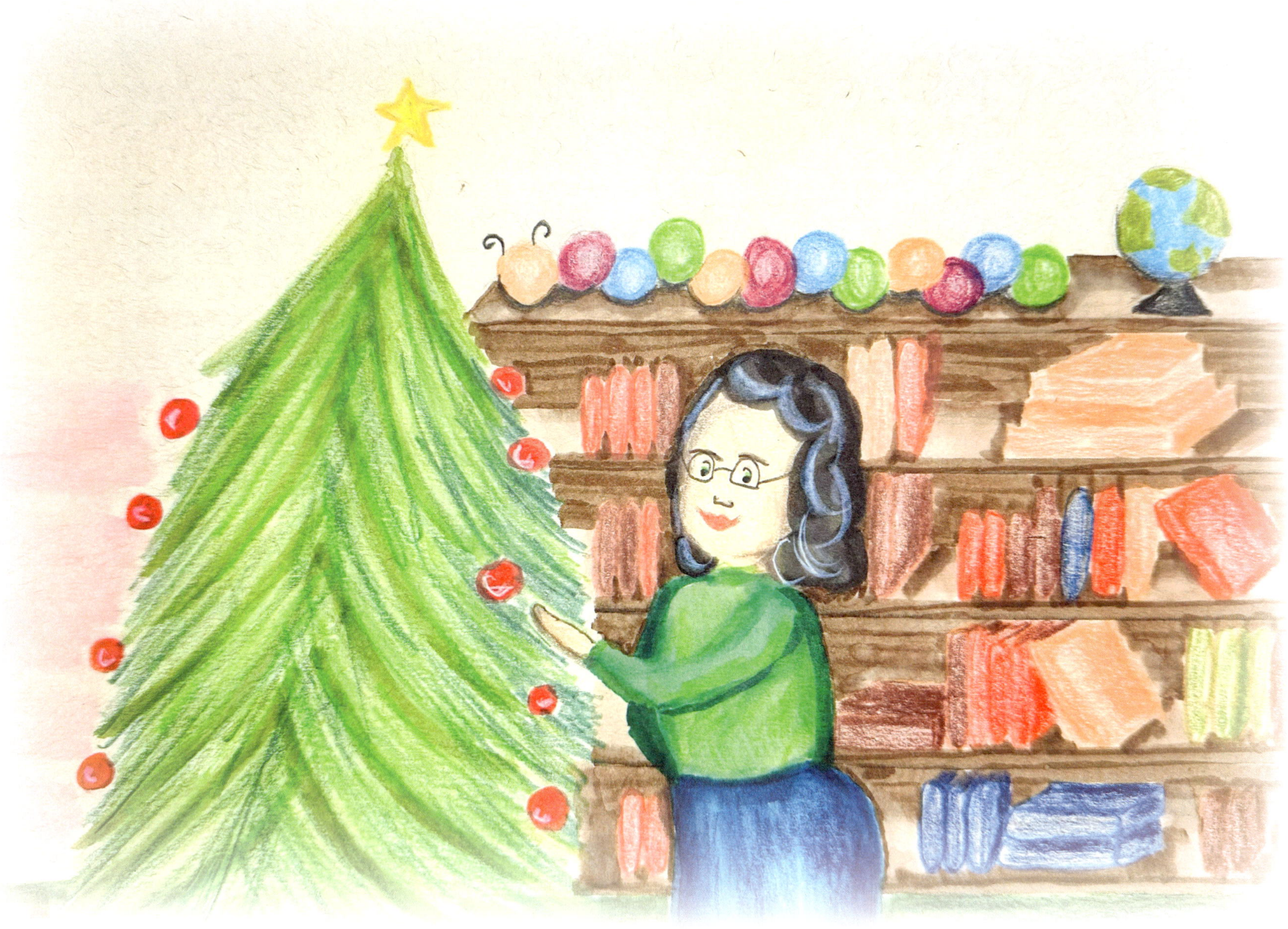

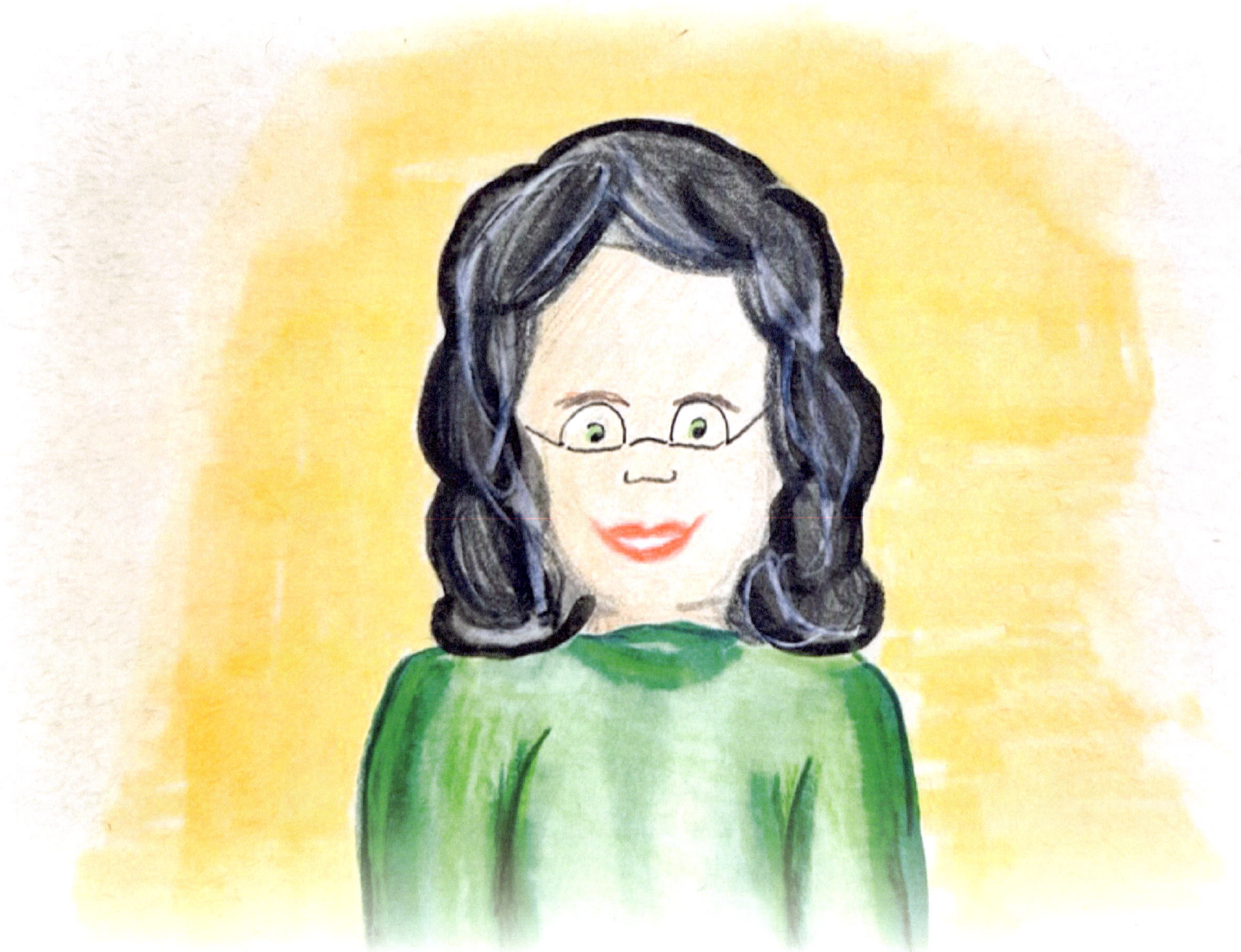

As Ms. Diaz entered the store, the pleasant smells and happy sounds instantly returned the smile to her face. As she turned the corner, her eyes saw the colorful racks of clothes, and her purpose for coming to the store was renewed—she didn't stop to look around; she knew exactly where she was going.

In fact, Ms. Diaz was so focused on her task that she never even noticed that another one of her students had seen her out and about!

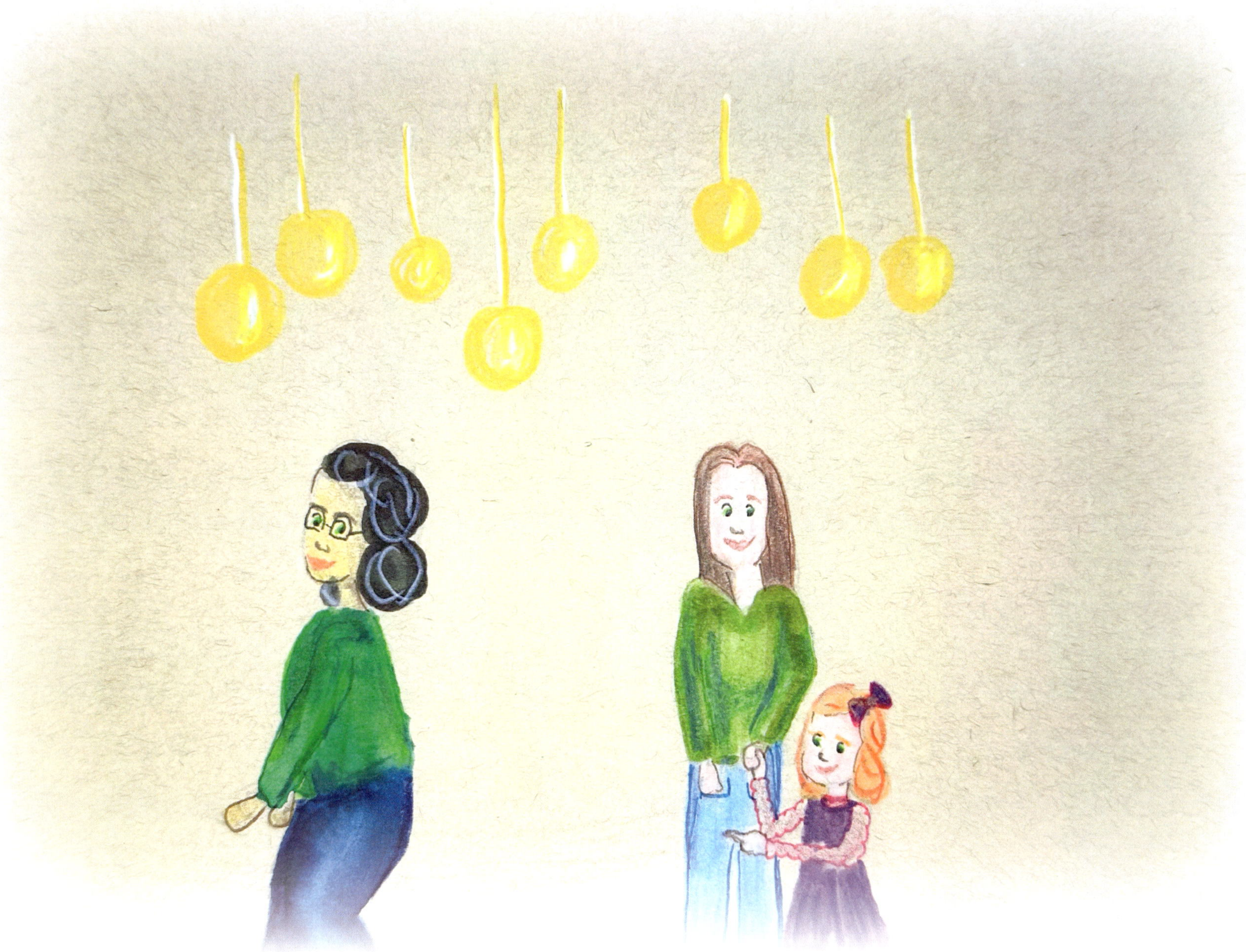

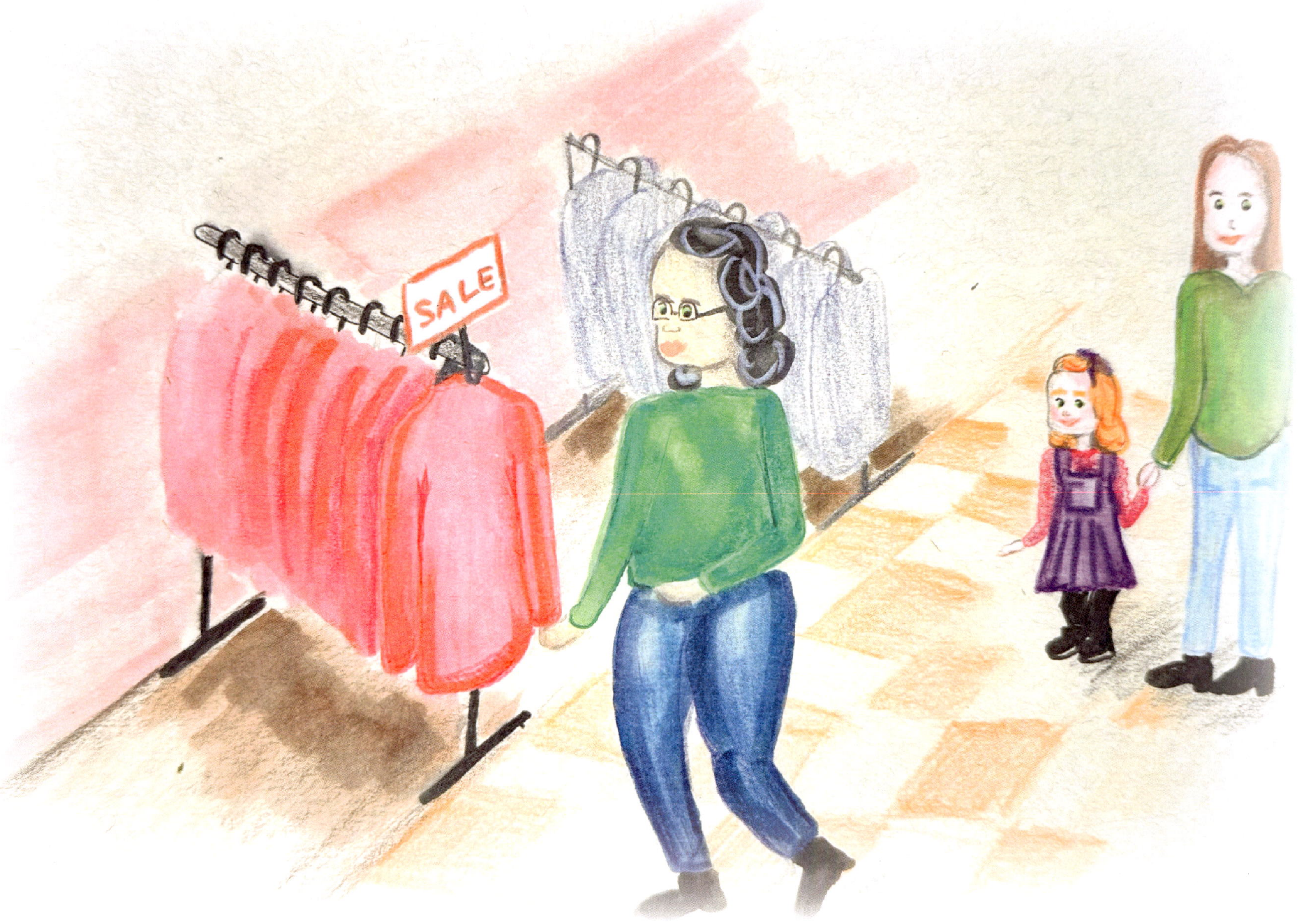
SALE

On the corner rack of the ladies' department, there was the beautiful sweater she'd been admiring all season. Surprisingly, it was on sale, and her size was still available. Ms. Diaz could not believe her luck! Thinking about how nice she'd look tomorrow in the new sweater, she picked it up and walked around the corner towards the check-out to make her purchase.

Ms. Diaz was almost at the register when her eyes happened to spy on something in the kid's department that caught her attention. She left the line and went to get a closer look.

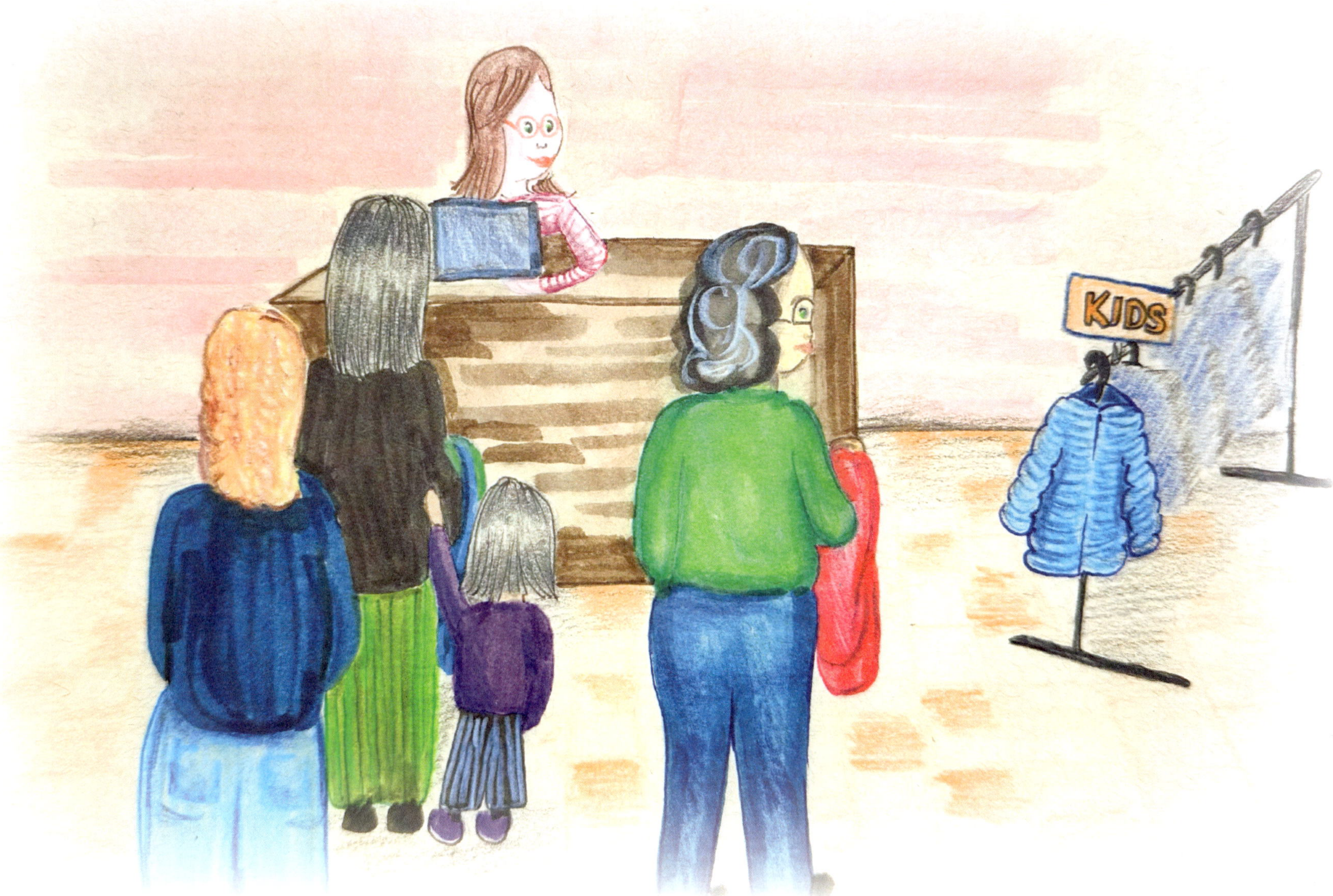
KIDS

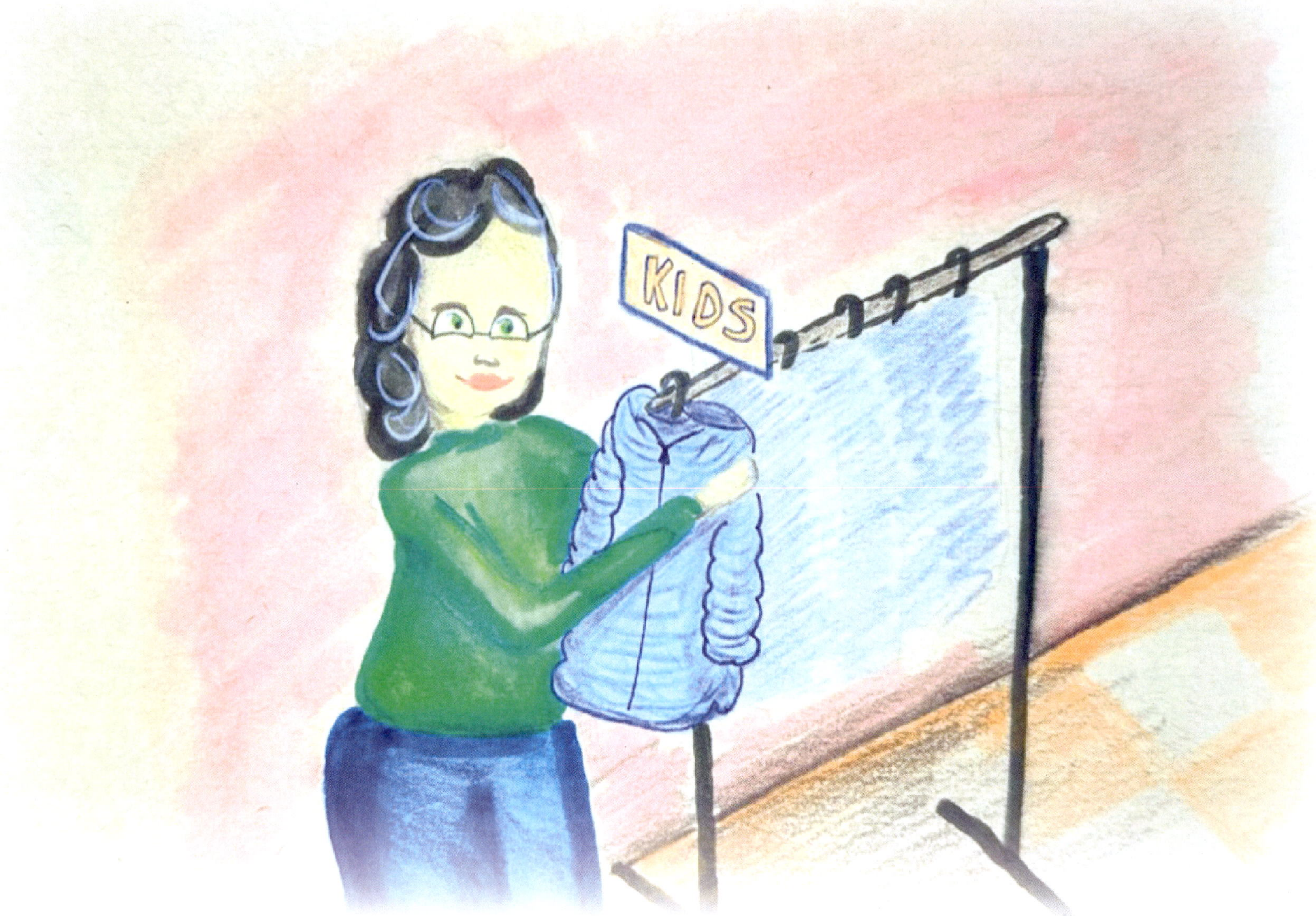
KIDS

As she gazed at the item, her thoughts returned to her classroom and one exceptional student. Her mind was made up instantly—though she came to that store for a specific thing, she left with something else entirely.

The next day at school, there was an eager excitement in the air as it was the last day before winter break. The children all dressed cheerily and brought gifts and treats—all that is, except for Nicholas.

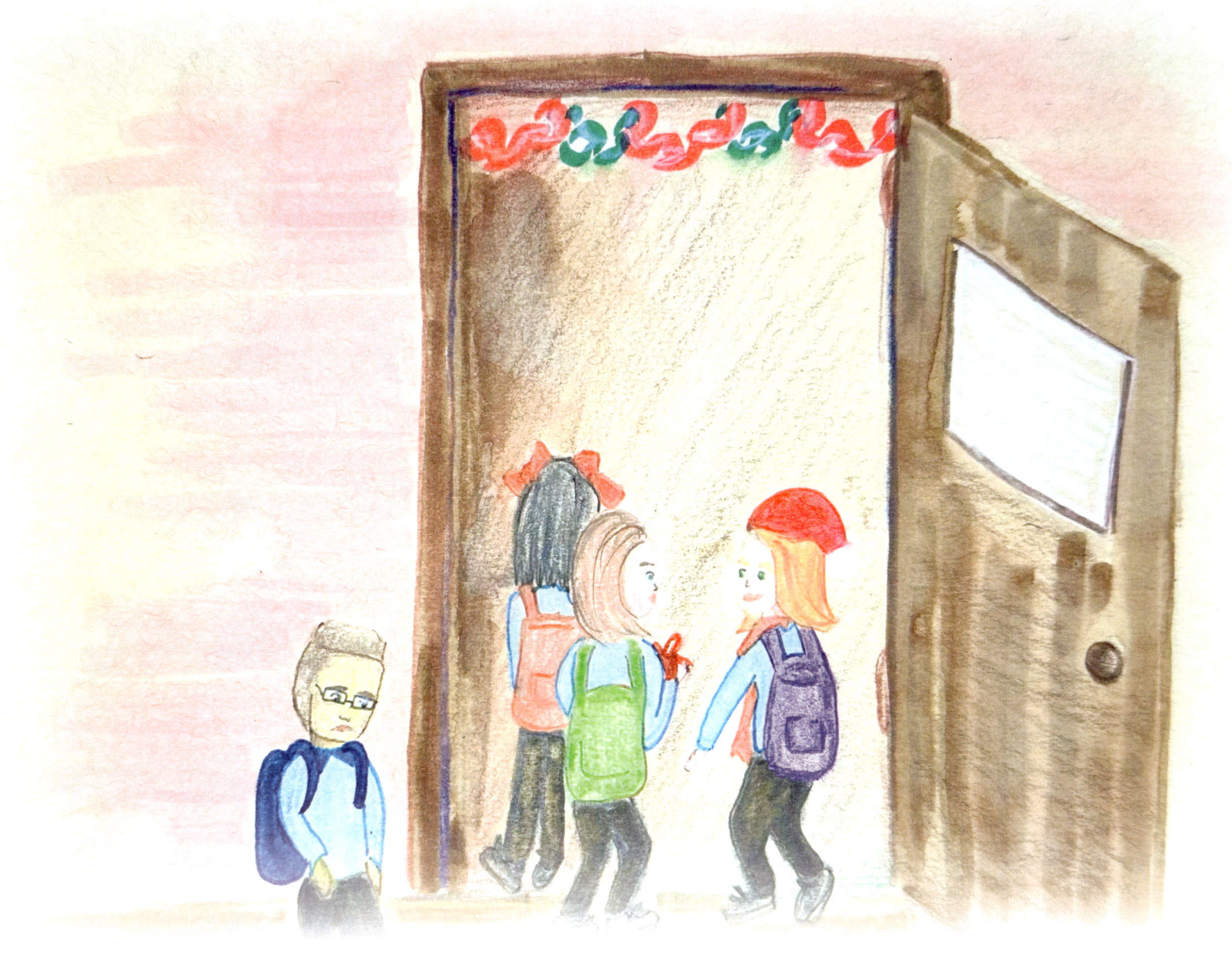

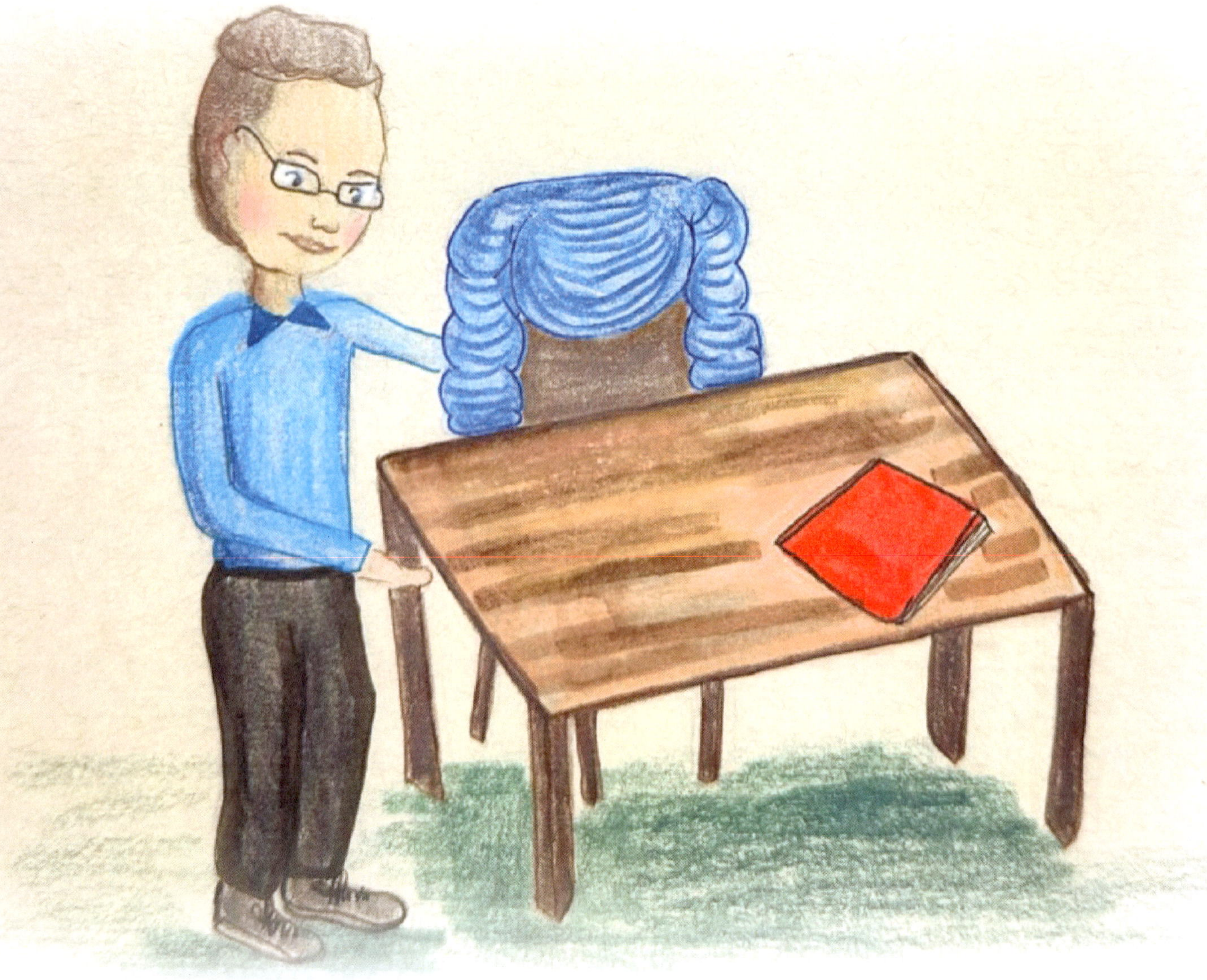

Nicholas wasn't wearing shiny clothes, nor did he bring cookies and candy like the other students—he just came to school like it was any other day. While the other students were hanging up their coats, Nicholas walked to his desk and was surprised to see a strange coat hanging on the back of his chair.

Confused, he looked around to see if someone had accidentally set their coat at the wrong desk. As Ms. Diaz approached him, she carefully chose her words and said, "This must be yours, Nicholas. No one else in our class is missing a coat."

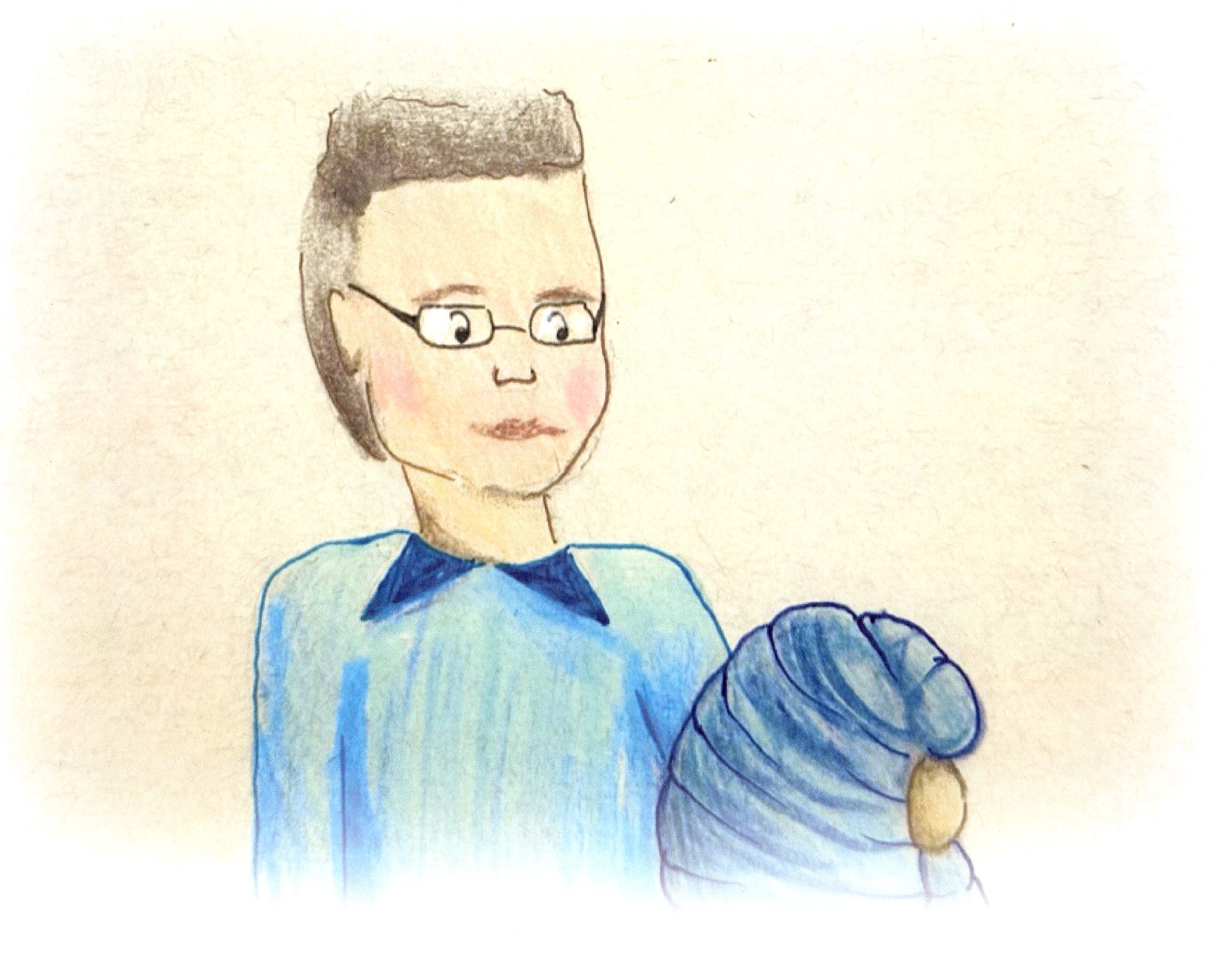

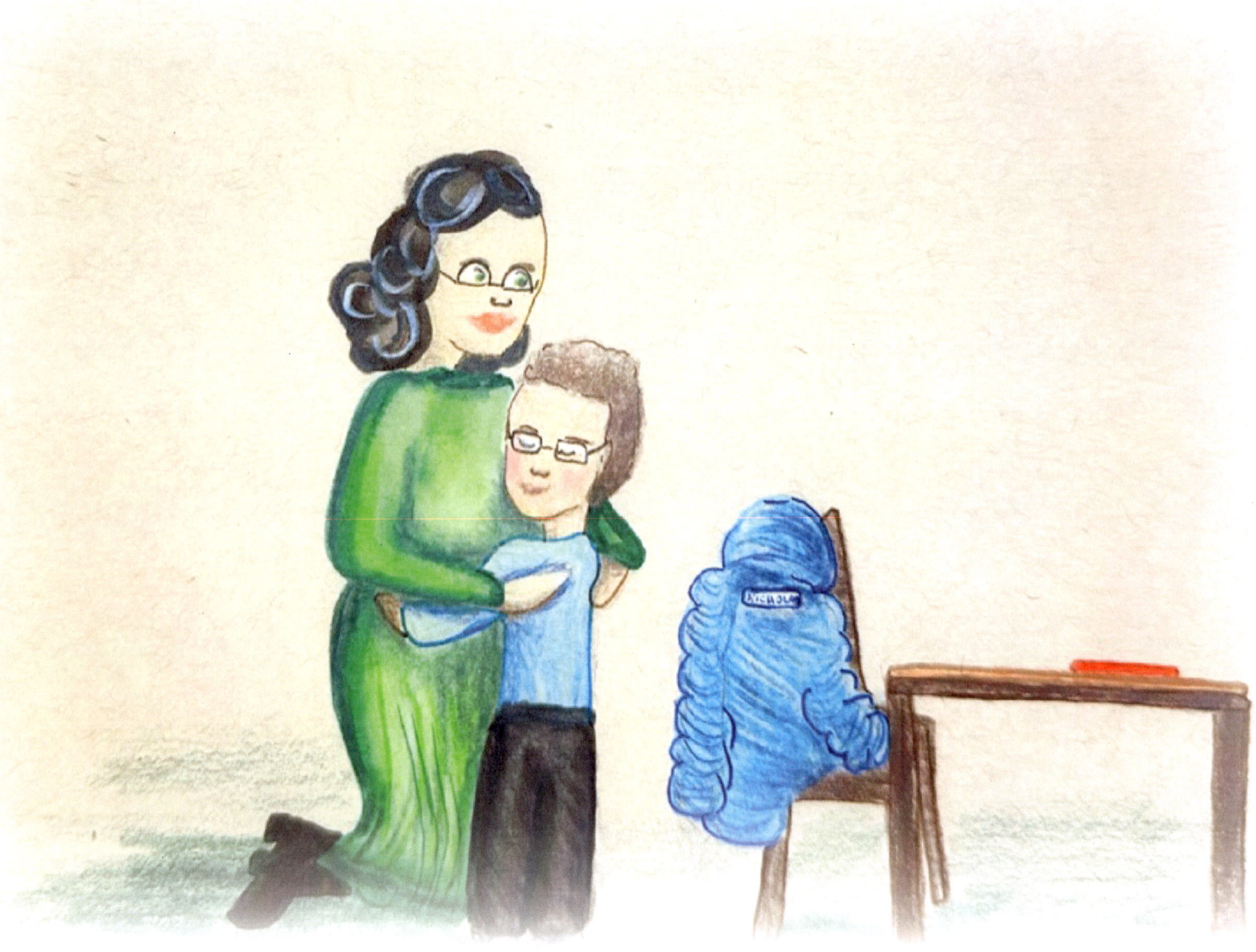

Nicholas looked at the coat and then at Ms. Diaz—he tried to tell her it wasn't his, but she showed him his name right there, hand-stitched inside the coat. He looked at the stitching of his name inside the coat, and then, with a sudden realization, he looked up at his teacher. As tears ran down his cheeks, he hugged Ms. Diaz. "Oh, thank you! Thank you very much!" He exclaimed.

That day, Nicholas got to go outside to play and even made a snowman with his classmates. Ms. Diaz was on recess duty and seemed even happier than usual.

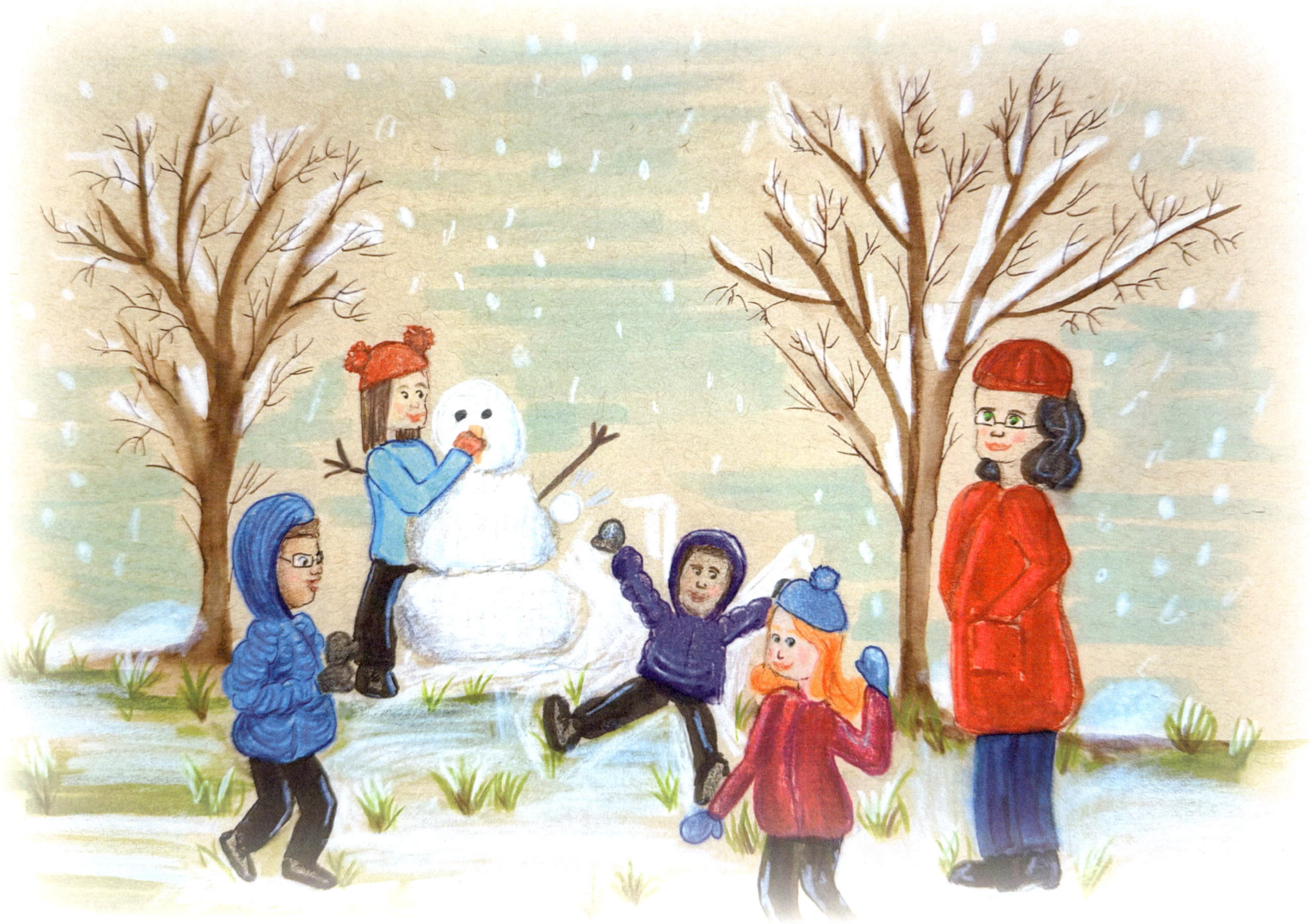

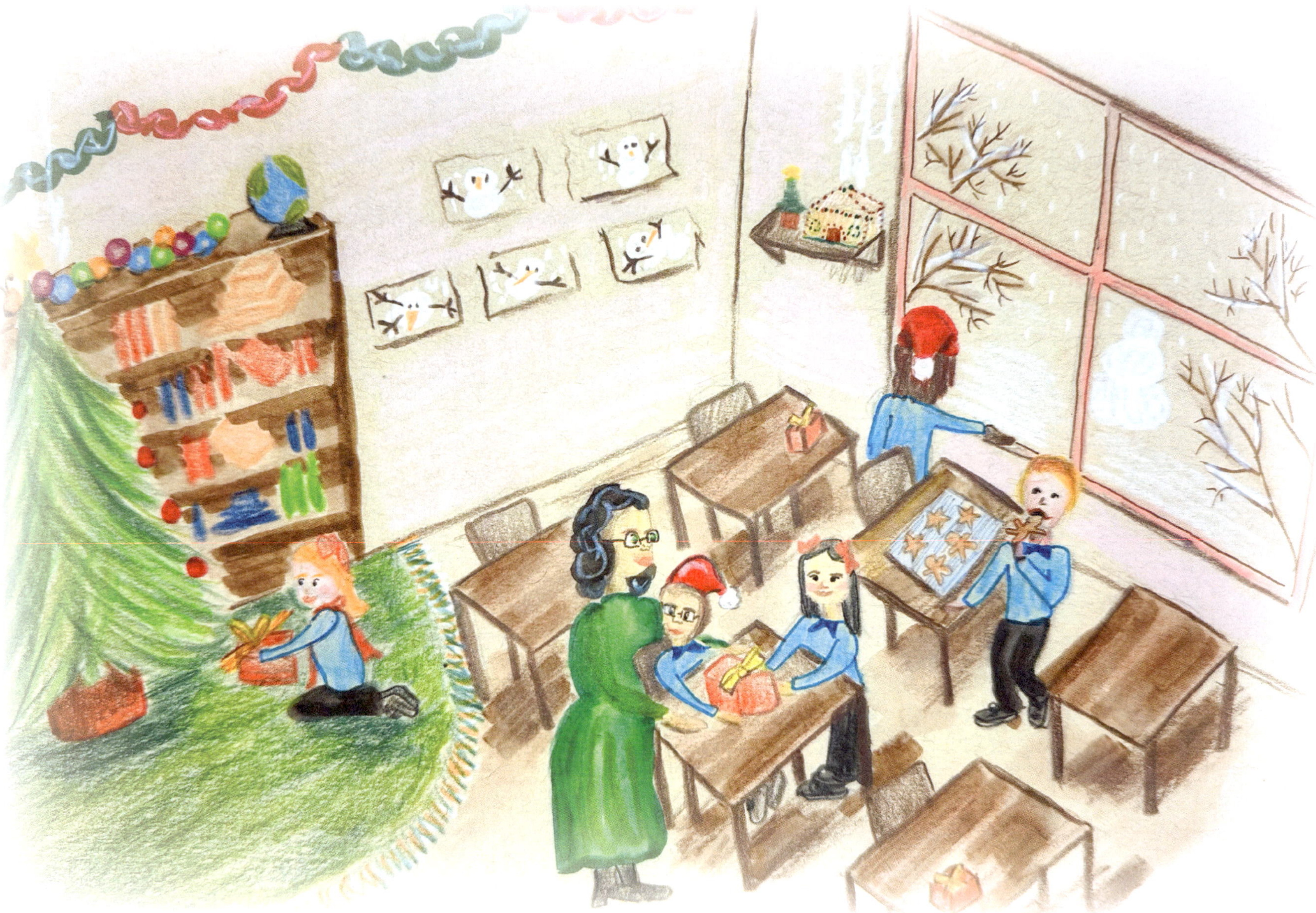

After recess, the students came back inside for their class party. They decorated cookies to look like snowmen, sang songs, made crafts, and gave gifts to each other—they all had a wonderful time.

At the end of the day, after all the students had left, Ms. Diaz cleaned the classroom. She turned on her holiday music and became busy picking up, feeling very pleased with how the day had gone.

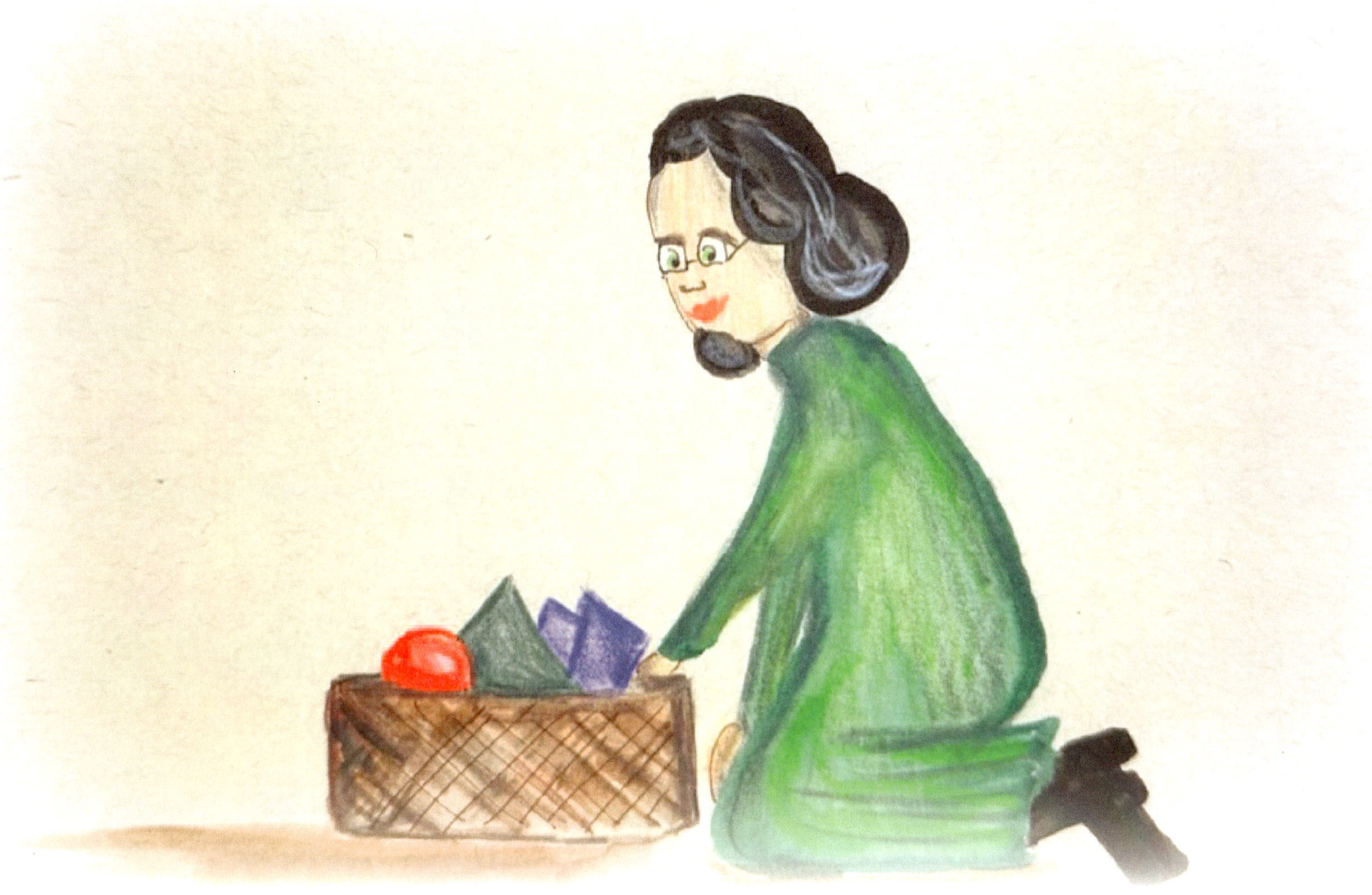

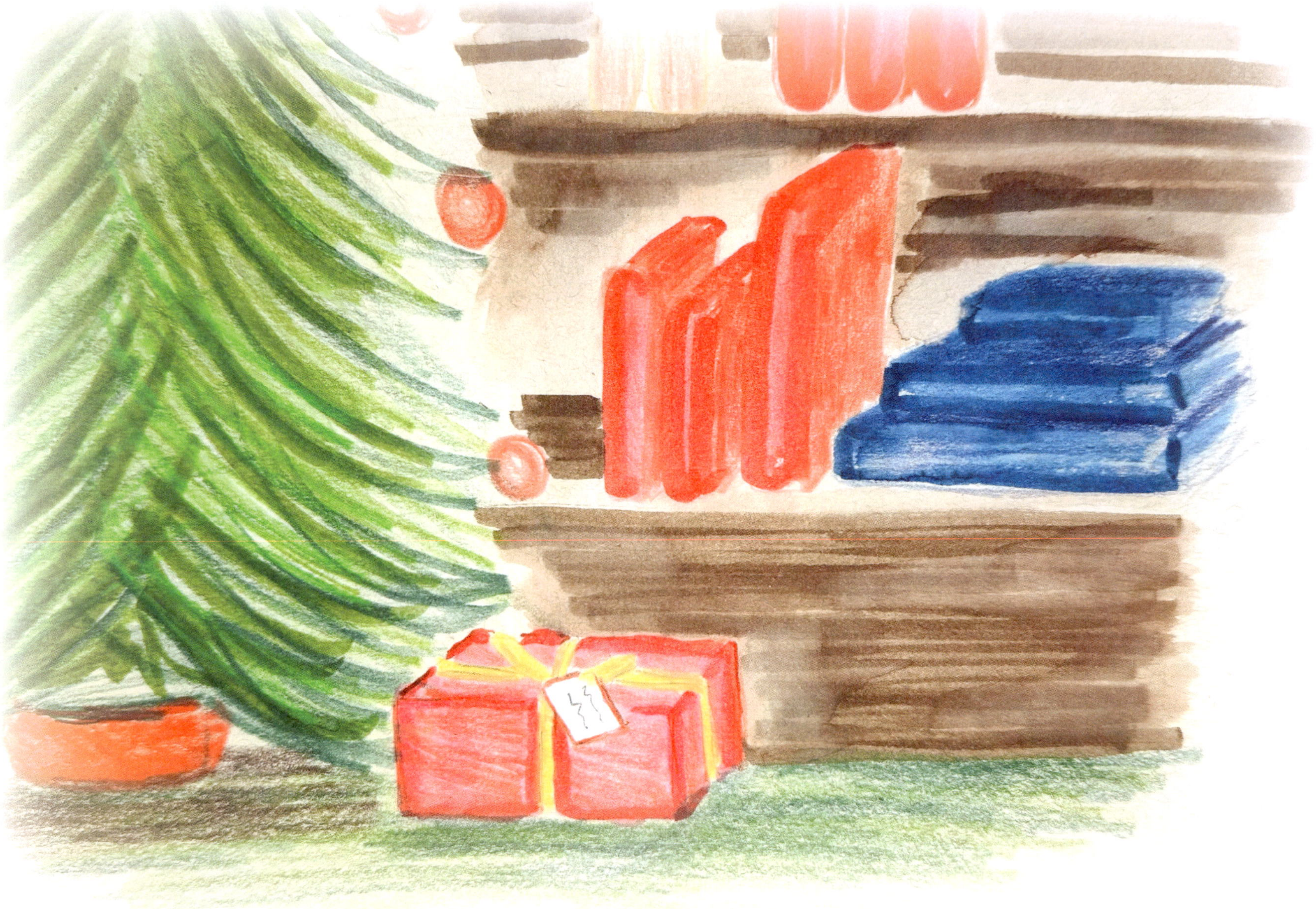

As she finished, she noticed a gift still left under the tree. She picked up the present and saw her name on the tag, but it did not say who it was from.

Ms. Diaz opened the present and was astonished to see that inside the box was the sweater she had wanted all season—the exact sweater she planned to purchase the day before.

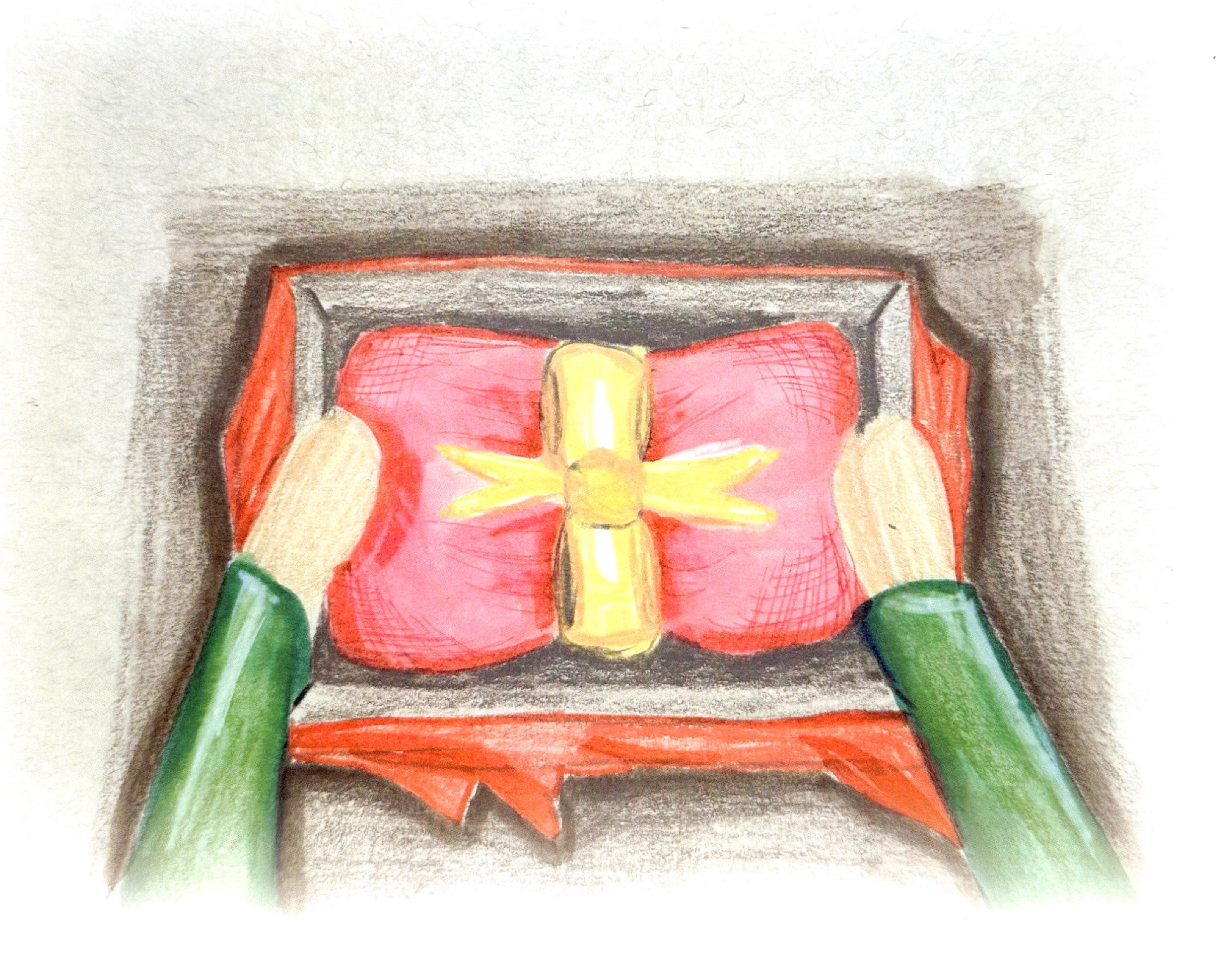

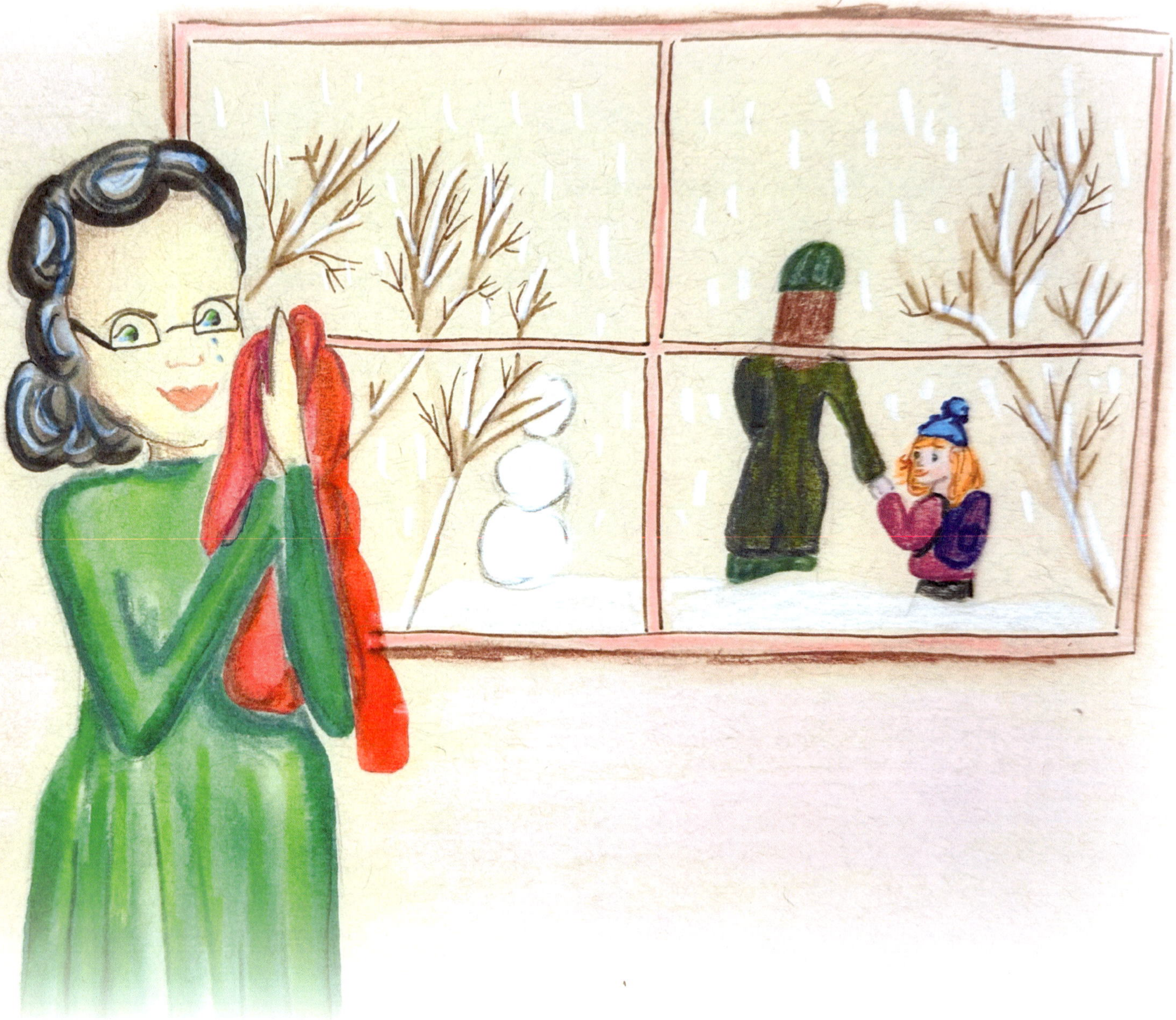

This time, it was Ms. Diaz's turn to have tears in her eyes. She had so many feelings: feelings of gratitude, happiness, and love. Looking at her gift, she reflected on how lucky she was to be a teacher and work every day doing what she loves with such remarkable children.

The End

Milton Keynes UK
Ingram Content Group UK Ltd.
UKRC041402201123
432910UK00001B/2